WORKBOOK FOR THE BODY KEEPS THE SCORE

BRAIN, MIND, AND BODY IN THE HEALING OF TRAUMA

By

Bessel van der Kolk M.D.

JESSICA RHODES

ISBN: 978-1-63809-019-9

Table of Contents

HOW TO USE THIS WORKBOOK

The goal of this workbook is to help people of different ages, genders, races, cultures, and boundaries to see the world in a different light that is free from trauma. This will happen as individuals attempt to answer the questions in this book sincerely, and carry out the exercises.

The lessons learned from each chapter bring to the fore important points that are essential for the integration of the different parts of the self. This will correct the wrong perceptions that the reader has in the long run.

Before answering the questions, it is advised that you make more than one copy of this workbook. Re-attempt to answer these questions after two or three months, and you will notice that there are improvements in the way your mind works.

Don't be too hard on yourself when answering the questions. If the questions or tasks feel too difficult, leave it and come back to it when you feel better. Make sure you're relaxed as you answer these questions.

INTRODUCTION

Your body keeps the score by Bessel Van Der Kolk has been written to help those who suffer from trauma to get over the distressing effects of trauma. It also gives family members, friends, therapists, and caregivers a peek into the lives of these individuals so they can understand the sufferers better.

The author gives informed and practical insight into the different approaches to get over the effects of trauma that is meant to mend the brain, mind, and body. The approaches in this workbook are meant to help every individual recover, rebound, and live their lives meaningfully and happily.

PART ONE: THE REDISCOVERY OF TRAUMA

CHAPTER ONE: LESSONS FROM VIETNAM VETERANS

Here are a few points from this chapter

People who suffer from Traumatic Neuroses, which is also called posttraumatic stress disorder (PTSD), develop a chronic vigilance for and sensitivity to threat. Trauma, whether it is the result of something done to you or something you have done, makes it difficult to engage in an intimate relationship. After you have experienced something so unspeakable, how do you learn to trust yourself or anyone else again? How do you surrender to an intimate relationship after you have been brutally violated?

Imagination is absolutely critical to the quality of our lives. It allows us to leave our routine everyday existence by fantasizing about travel, food, sex, falling in love, or having the last word. It will enable envisioning new possibilities, and it is an essential launchpad for making our hopes come true. This is the part that is affected after a trauma.

Traumatized people look at the world in a fundamentally different way from other people.

For people who go through trauma, they can get stuck as the event that caused them so much pain had also become their sole source of meaning. They felt fully alive when they were revisiting their traumatic past.

Trauma isn't just an event that took place sometime in the past; it is also the imprint left by that experience on the mind, brain, and body.

For real change to take place, the body needs to learn that the danger has passed and to live in the reality of the present.

Please answer the following questions

1. You lose a part of your mind, body, and brain when you experience trauma. True **or** False
2. It is impossible to find yourself in an intimate relationship after trauma. True **or** False
3. The mind knows the trauma has passed for you to move on with your life. True **or** False
4. How can trauma influence or affect your imagination?

____

____

____

____

____

____

5. Do you know someone who has experienced trauma? Yes **or** No
6. How easily does the person have a change in mood? What happens that makes the person burst out in rage or anger?

____

____

____

____

____

____

7. What is the sign of change or improvement you would see to determine if you have made progress? Will it be getting closer to your family? Talking about the event freely? Controlling your anger? Mention them

____

____

____

____

CHAPTER TWO: REVOLUTIONS IN UNDERSTANDING MIND AND BRAIN

A few points we looked at in this chapter

More than half the people who seek psychiatric care have been assaulted, abandoned, neglected, or even raped as children or have witnessed violence in their families. People who were abused as children often feel sensations that have no physical cause.

Most human suffering is related to love and loss. Therapists are to help people acknowledge the experience and bear the reality of life withal its pleasures and heartbreak.

The most significant sources of our sufferings are the lies we tell ourselves. People can never get better without knowing what they know and feeling what they feel.

Healing is a matter of experiential knowledge. You can be fully in charge of your life only if you can acknowledge the reality of your body in all its visceral dimensions

Psychiatric medications have a severe downside as they may deflect attention from dealing with underlying issues.

Our capacity to destroy one another is matched by our ability to heal one another. Restoring relationships and community is central to restoring well-being

Language gives us the power to change ourselves and others by communicating our experiences, helping us define what we know, and finding a shared sense of meaning.

We can change social conditions to create environments in which children and adults can feel safe and where they can thrive.

Answer the following questions as sincerely as possible.

1. Do you hallucinate? Yes **or** No
2. Do you think it is connected to an event in your past?

Yes **or** No

3. Do you feel pain from an event in the past? Yes **or** No
4. You can only get better when you can acknowledge what you know and feel.
   True **or** False
5. Relationships and community are essential for the well-being of individuals. True **or** False
6. For traumatized people, re-exposure to stress might provide a similar relief from anxiety. True **or** False
7. A professor felt relaxed only when he felt his wife's bum. What actions (that may seem weird to everyone) from others have helped you feel loved or satisfied with your need?

____
____
____
____
____
____

8. Do you feel better when you speak about what you feel concerning a trauma? Explain your reason.

____
____
____
____
____
____

9. How do drugs or medication make you feel?

____
____
____
____
____
____

10. If you had your way, would you take out medication from your treatment or recovery process? If yes, why, if no, why not?

11. What other options make you feel better? Social gatherings, speaking to someone you love, talking to someone who understands and can empathize? Mention them

CHAPTER THREE: LOOKING INTO THE BRAIN: THE NEUROSCIENCE REVOLUTION

A few points we looked at in this chapter

When traumatized people are presented with images, sounds, or thoughts related to their particular experience, the amygdala (the part of the brain that warns us of impending danger) reacts with alarm. This triggers stress hormones and impulses that drive up blood pressure, heart rate, and oxygen intake, preparing the body for fight or flight.

Traumatized people have enormous difficulty telling other people what happened to them. Their bodies experience terror, rage, and helplessness as well as the impulse to flight or free, but these feelings are almost impossible to articulate.

The stress hormones of traumatized people take much longer to return to baseline, and it spikes quickly and disproportionately in response to mildly stressful stimuli. Constantly elevated stress hormones lead to memory and attention problems, irritability, and sleep disorders.

The two halves of the brain speak different languages. The right side is intuitive, emotional, visual, spatial, and tactual. It communicates through facial expression and body language. The left side is in charge of talking. It is activated when children begin to speak and express their unique experiences to others.

Some people go into denial when faced with a threat. The mind may learn to ignore the messages from the emotional brain as this brain keeps working while stress hormones keep sending signals to the muscles to tense for action or immobilize in collapse. The effects are unabated until they demand notice by falling ill. No matter how much insight and understanding we develop, the rational brain is impotent to talk the emotional brain out of its reality

Talking about trauma can be used to dissolve distressing feelings about them. The experience of the trauma itself can get in the way of doing that.

Answer the following questions truthfully

1. Cast your mind back to an event that caused you trauma. How do you feel about it? What emotions do you experience when you think about it?

____

____

____

____

____

____

2. When you cast your mind back to an event that caused you trauma, can you get over it immediately like nothing happened or like you're moving on? If yes, why, and if no, why not?

____

____

____

____

____

____

3. When you remember an event that caused trauma, how do you manage through it? Is it by drinking, drugs, smoking, eating, excessive workout? Mention them

____

____

____

____

____

____

4. Do you visit a therapist? Yes **or** No
5. Does it help? Yes **or** No
6. Stress hormones are triggered when events, images, words, or sounds relating to the trauma happen. True **or** False
7. The two sides of the brain have different functions. True False
8. How can you be here and not there? How can you be in the present and not linger in the shadow of the trauma? What can you do to make things better? Talking about the experience, joining a rehabilitation program? Visiting a therapist? Mention them

____

____

____

____

____

____

PART TWO: THIS IS YOUR BRAIN ON TRAUMA

CHAPTER FOUR: RUNNING FOR YOUR LIFE: THE ANATOMY OF SURVIVAL

A few points we looked at in this chapter

Traumatized people become stuck, stopped in their growth because they can't integrate new experiences into their lives. Being traumatized means continuing to organize your life as if the trauma were still going on – unchanged and immutable – as every new encounter is contaminated by the past.

Healing from PTSD means being able to terminate this continued stress mobilization and restore the entire organism to safety.

If you want to manage your emotions better, your brain gives you two options: you can learn to regulate them from top-down or from the bottom up. You can regulate them from the top down or the bottom up.

Top-down involves strengthening the capacity of the watchtower to monitor your meditations. Mindfulness meditation and yoga can help with this. Bottom up-regulation involves recalibrating the autonomic nervous system. Breathing exercises can help with this.

Psychologists help people use insight and understanding to manage their behavior, while neuroscience research shows that very few psychological problems are as a result of defects in understanding. Most originate in pressures from deeper regions in the brain that drive our perception and attention.

Dissociation is the essence of trauma as it makes the experience split off and fragmented so that emotions, sounds, images, thoughts, and physical sensations related to the trauma take a life of their own. These fragments intrude into the present and are relived.

Once the trauma isn't resolved, the stress hormones that the body secretes to protect itself keep circulating, and the defensive movements and emotional responses keep getting replayed. Therapy won't work as long as people are being pulled back into the past.

Answer the following questions as sincerely as you can. Try out the exercises as well.

1. There are three parts of our brain. True **or** False
2. Do you think you relive your trauma? Yes **or** No
3. I find it difficult to get close or intimate with people or the present because I fear or I'm prepared for the trauma in my past. Yes **or** No
4. The brain is tasked with our survival. True **or** False
5. Emotions can't assign value to experiences, and this is the foundation of reason. True **or** False
6. Can you mention the last thing, action, or event that triggered stress for you? While doing it, can you also take note of the things going on around you? Take note of the colors, flowers, and everything happening in the present and write it out.

____

____

____

____

____

____

7. Would you describe yourself as someone who overreacts to an issue?

____

____

____

8. When you react, do you shut down on your own naturally, or you need the help of alcohol, drugs, and other things to help you shut down, or do you feel numb?

____
____
____
____
____
____

9. Do you feel more inclined to sadness, or do you easily block out pleasure and joy?

____
____
____

10. What would you do to become better in one year? Acupressure, rhythmic interactions, drumming, dancing, or playing ball at the beach? Mention them

____
____
____
____
____
____

11. Pick up a journal and write out events that have led to your trauma. Write out these events in 30 days. Be factual about it and keep it out from the sight and reach for everyone.

CHAPTER FIVE: BODY- BRAIN CONNECTIONS

A few points we looked at in this chapter

As long as the mind is defending itself against invincible assaults, our closest bonds are threatened along with our ability to imagine, play, plan, learn, and pay attention to other people's needs.

Being able to feel safe with other people is probably the single most crucial aspect of mental health; safe connections are fundamental to meaningful and satisfying lives. Social support isn't just staying in the midst of others but also reciprocity, which is being truly heard and seen by the people around us, feeling that we are held in someone else's mind and heart.

It is normal for mammals to always be on guard. To get close to another human being emotionally, our defensive system has to shut down temporarily. Traumatized individuals can either be too hyper-vigilant to enjoy the ordinary pleasures that life has to offer, or they can be too numb to be alert to signs of real danger.

If the memory of trauma is encoded in the viscera, in heartbreaking and gut-wrenching emotions, in autoimmune disorders and skeletal/muscular problems, and if mind/brain/visceral communication is the royal road to emotion regulation, this demands a radical shift in our therapeutic assumptions.

Answer the following questions as sincerely as you can

1. Do you feel lonely even when you find yourself in the midst of people? Yes **or** No
2. The sympathetic nervous system is charged with arousal. True **or** False
3. The VVC works with the sympathetic and parasympathetic nervous systems.
   True **or** False

4. Do you feel calm and safe when the important people in your life listen to you?
   Yes **or** No
5. Immobilization is at the root of trauma. True **or** False
6. What other things make you feel calm and safe? Is it singing, yoga, keeping a pet, breathing exercises? Mention them.

____

____

____

____

____

____

7. When faced with life-threatening situations, what do you do? Panic, scream and get into fear and/or rage, or shut down and become dead to everything around you? Mention what you do.

____

____

____

____

____

____

8. What steps do you think you can take to help you get over a trauma? Breathing exercises, martial arts, yoga, group singing, and/or dancing? Mention them

____

____

____

____

____

____

CHAPTER SIX: LOSING YOUR BODY, LOSING YOUR SELF

A few points we looked at in this chapter

Chronic emotional abuse and neglect can be just as devastating as physical abuse and sexual molestation.

In response to trauma and in coping with the dread that persisted long afterward, trauma victims shut down the parts of the brain that transmit visceral feelings and emotions that accompany and define terror. Their relationship with their inner reality has been impaired.

Our minds act as a screen, not just to discover facts but also to hide them. Knowing what we feel is the first step to understanding why we feel them.

The gut feelings signal what is safe, life-threatening, or sustainable even when we can't explain why we feel a particular way.

The more people try to push away and ignore internal warning signs, the more likely the feelings can take over and leave them bewildered, confused, and ashamed. People who cannot comfortably notice what is going on inside become vulnerable to any sensory shift either by shutting down or by going into a panic. They develop a fear of fear itself.

Alexithymia is when you don't have words for feelings. People with this condition register their emotions as physical problems rather than as signals that something deserves their attention. They don't know how they feel.

Trauma victims can't recover until they become familiar with and befriend the sensations in their bodies.

To have genuine relationships, you have to be able to experience others as separate individuals, each with his or her particular motivations and intentions. While you need to be able to stand up for yourself, you also need to recognize that other people have their own agendas. Trauma makes the line between them hazy.

Answer the following questions as sincerely as possible

1. Extreme disconnection means you lose track of yourself and everything around you. True **or** False
2. When your brain is focused on trauma, it can't focus on you. True **or** False
3. The brain has a choice of whether to monitor and evaluate the environment.
   True **or** False
4. Do you ever get out of trouble only to find yourself in some kind of trouble or trauma again? Yes **or** No
5. Can you sense when you shouldn't approach a person or place? What do you do when you sense this feeling?

____

____

____

____

____

____

6. Do your emotions have more to say when certain events happen? Do you lack the words to describe how you feel immediately an event happens? Do you suddenly develop diarrhea, and later you find out it was because you were in a state of panic? Cite an example

____

____

____

____

____

____

7. Pay attention to the times you get angry and try to notice if you're merely frustrated or really angry.
8. Think back to an event that happened to you that didn't bother you. Looking back, how do you feel about the event? Diarrhea, anger, tightness in the chest, or gnawing in your belly? Mention them

____

____

____

____

____

____

9. What skills can help you handle distressing emotions better? How can you get better? By therapy, massage, acupuncture or acupressure, cling to someone else, breathing exercises, yoga? Mention them

____

____

____

____

____

____

PART THREE: THE MINDS OF CHILDREN

CHAPTER SEVEN: GETTING ON THE SAME WAVELENGTH: ATTACHMENT AND ATTUNEMENT

A few points we learned in this chapter

For abused children, the whole world is filled with triggers.

A mother's love and presence are important in the life of a child. If a mother can't meet her baby's impulses and needs, the baby learns to become the mother's idea of what the baby is.

Children get in sync with their environment and with the people around them and develop self-awareness, empathy, impulse control, and self-motivation that make it possible to become contributing members of the larger social culture.

Children get attached to their primary caregiver. When the attachment is secure, then the caregiver involves emotional atonement to their role.

We soothe newborns, but parents soon start teaching their children to tolerate higher levels of arousal, a job that is often assigned to fathers. Associating intense sensations with safety, comfort, and mastery is the foundation of self-regulation, self-soothing, and self-nurture.

Children who lack physical atonement are vulnerable to shutting down the direct feedback from their bodies, the seat of pleasure, purpose, and direction. Kids will go to almost any length to feel seen and connected.

Attachment patterns continue into adulthood. Anxious children become anxious adults, and they become bullied. Avoidant children become adults who are out of touch with their feelings and those of others as they bully others.

Dissociation means simultaneously knowing or not knowing. If you cannot tolerate what you know or feel, the only option is denial and dissociation. You don't feel real inside and then resort to extremes to feel something.

Answer the following questions as sincerely as you can

1. Imitation is a fundamental social skill. True **or** False
2. Without the internal locus of control, the child will be able to learn healthy coping throughout life. True **or** False
3. As a child, did you get bullied or did you bully someone?

____

4. If you were bullied, were you usually anxious as a child? What was childhood like for you? Were you always frightened?

____

____

____

____

____

____

5. If you bullied someone, did you feel numb to your emotions as a child? What was childhood like for you? Were you barely noticed? Did you feel loved?

____

____

____

____

____

____

6. As a child, what was your relationship with your parents like? Did they have time for you? Did you feel loved, or did you live in fear?

____
____
____
____
____
____

7. Do you feel alive when you're faced with potentially dangerous situations?
   Yes **or** No
8. Do you think people treat you horribly, and your parents did the same because you are a terrible person? Yes **or** No
9. Do you think your mother loved you? Why?

____
____
____
____
____
____

10. How do you think you can get better? Hugs, learning to laugh and smile with others, expressing delight and disapproval at the right moment, joining a choir or a dance group or band or basketball team? Mention them

____
____
____
____
____
____

CHAPTER EIGHT: TRAPPED IN RELATIONSHIPS: THE COST OF ABUSE AND NEGLECT

A few points we learned in this chapter

People with a history of incest have their immune system oversensitive to threats, so they are defensive when it isn't necessary even if it means attacking their body cells. It has a problem knowing when to feel safe because the past is impressed in their minds as misinterpretations of innocuous events.

People who go through abuse and neglect have their own view of how the world functions.

People who go through childhood trauma and incest can be changed during adolescence when the brain once again goes through a period of exponential change.

Change begins when we learn to own our emotional brains, when we learn to observe and tolerate the heartbreaking and gut-wrenching sensations that register misery and humiliation. After learning to bear what's going on inside, can we start to befriend not obliterate our emotions that keep our maps fixed and immutable.

People who go through trauma are involved in soul murder, which is erasing awareness and cultivating denial to survive, but you lose track of who you are, what you're feeling, and who you can trust.

Answer the following questions sincerely and try out the exercises

1. Our maps of the world are encoded in the emotional brain, and changing them means having to reorganize that part of the central nervous system. True **or** False

2. With fear, the rational brain takes charge of the emotional brain. True **or** False
3. Even though there are bad events that lead to trauma, do you believe there are good people who are out there who can help you change your narrative? If yes, why? If no, why not?

____

____

____

____

____

____

4. Which of the following statements is rational to you?
   - I am the problem that's why wrong people are drawn towards me
   - I was abused, but it wasn't my fault
   - The world has both good and bad people in it
   - I can never be good enough to be loved
5. Do you sometimes feel caved in by your feelings? Do you feel overwhelmed until you act on what you feel? Yes **or** No
6. Did you always wish you had another family from the one you grew up in? Yes **or** No
7. What can help you get over these feelings? Breathing exercises, mindfulness, acupressure? Mention them

____

____

____

____

____

____

8. Try to make a drawing about an event that triggered trauma for you. Show the picture to your therapist or a happy child and ask them what they see when they look at the picture. If their views are entirely different from yours, write it out and go over it later to see if it correlates to the picture.

CHAPTER NINE: WHAT'S LOVE GOT TO DO WITH IT

A few points we learned from this chapter

When children must disown compelling experiences they've had, this creates serious problems, including chronic distrust of other people, inhibition of curiosity, distrust of their own senses, and the tendency to find everything unreal.

Child abuse is a high-risk public health issue.

Psychotropic agents make abuse victims tractable but impair their ability to feel pleasure and maintain curiosity. Such people find it challenging to grow and develop emotionally, intellectually, and become contributing members of the society.

Answer the following questions sincerely

1. Do you find it challenging to concentrate? Are you easily angered and filled with self-loathing? Yes **or** No
2. Treating child abuse is costlier than cancer or heart disease in the long run. True **or** False
3. Did you go through trauma and abuse as a child?
   Yes **or** No
4. Have you ever visited a therapist or psychologist or anyone who could offer help? Yes **or** No
5. Did you feel they couldn't connect with you or they weren't really interested or they weren't interested? Yes **or** No
6. Can you describe one of such experiences?

____

____

____

____

____

____

7. Tick the ones that apply to you

- I binge eat
- I'm an alcohol addict
- I smoke compulsively
- I abuse drugs or substances
- I get depressed very easily
- I'm overweight
- I get suicidal

8. If you ticked one or more of these boxes, were you abused as a child? Yes **or** No
9. Child abuse is one of the gravest and most costly public health issues in the United States. True **or** False
10. There's no link between child abuse and workplace performance. True **or** False

CHAPTER TEN: DEVELOPMENTAL TRAUMA: THE HIDDEN EPIDEMIC

A few points we learned in this chapter

We can only solve the problem in children if we correctly define what is going on with them and do more than developing new drugs to control them or trying to find the gene that is responsible for their disease. This is the only way to help them live productive lives.

Parents with their own genetic vulnerabilities can pass on that protection to the next generation provided they are given the right support.

The continued practice of applying multiple distinct co-morbid diagnoses to traumatized children has grave consequences: it defies parsimony, obscures etiological clarity, and runs the danger of relegating treatment and intervention to a small aspect of the child's psychopathology rather than promoting a comprehensive treatment approach.

Abused girls are more likely to go numb in the face of chronic stress and trauma. The girl may not even be aware, so she may not take protective action.

Answer the following questions sincerely

1. If you had a friend who was abused or faced trauma, would you advise him/her to a therapist or a support group, or get medication? Why?

____
____
____
____
____
____

2. Do you or do you know anyone who engages in chronic masturbation, self-harming activities, pulling out their hair, or picking at their skin till it bleeds? Yes **or** No
3. Do you know why?

____

____

____

____

____

____

4. Tick the boxes that correctly answer the question below.

Patients can be mislabeled when:

- There's no relationship between diagnosis and cure in a patient True **or** False
- When doctors can't agree on what ails their patients.

  True **or** False
- When patients prove to be stubborn

  True **or** False
- When patients argue with their doctors

  True **or** False
- When doctors want to be free

  True **or** False

5. Is it difficult for you to make and keep friends?
   Yes **or** No

6. If your answer is yes, do you think it Is because you overreact to slight frustrations or you feel despicable, and you loathe yourself, or you feel you aren't worth it? Mention the reasons

____

____

____

____

____

____

7. Wrongly diagnosing traumatized children can affect the child even as an adult.
   True **or** False
8. How can you become a better person before your next birthday? Social support, joining a choir, joining a basketball team? What else would you do? Mention them

____

____

____

____

____

____

PART FOUR: THE IMPRINT OF TRAUMA

CHAPTER ELEVEN: UNCOVERING SECRETS: THE PROBLEM OF TRAUMATIC MEMORY

A few points we learned in this chapter

When trauma occurs or when it is reactivated, the frontal lobe shuts down, including the region necessary to put feelings into words. This region creates our sense of location in time, and the thalamus, which integrates the raw data of incoming sensations and the emotional brain takes over even though the emotional brain isn't under conscious control so it can't communicate words.

The mind works according to schemes or maps, and events that are outside the norm gets our attention. If it's exciting news, we remember for a long time, but if it's insults and injuries, we remember this best. This is because the adrenaline that we secrete to defend against potential threats will imprint such memories into our minds. The more adrenaline you secrete, the more precise your memory will be. But if you are faced with horror, especially the horror of inescapable shock, the system becomes overwhelmed and breaks down.

Our ability to remember an event or incident accurately depends not only on how accurate our memories of it are but on how personally meaningful it was and how emotional we felt about it.

The imprints of traumatic experiences are organized not as coherent, logical narratives but in fragmented sensory and emotional traces as images, sounds, and physical sensations.

Trauma can be linked to hysteria, which is an emotional disorder that is characterized by emotional outbursts, susceptibility to suggestion and contractions, and paralysis of the muscles that can't be explained by a single anatomy.

There's a difference between narrative memory (what the traumatized person says about the trauma) and traumatic memory (precipitated by certain triggers).

Dissociation is the splitting off and isolation of memory imprints in people who suffer from trauma. The treatment is an association, which is integrating the cut-off elements of the trauma into the ongoing narrative of life so the brain can recognize that was then, this is now.

Answer the following questions as precisely as you can

1. Cast your mind back to a trauma you witnessed. Write down the date, the day of the week, and the time.

____

____

2. See if you can remember what happened at that same time on the day before the event occurred.

____

____

____

____

____

____

3. Is there someone you really dislike?

____

____

____

4. Do you know why?

____

____

____

____

5. Can you link the person to a trauma you experienced? Yes **or** No
6. Trauma is at the root of hysteria. True **or** False
7. Dissociation and association work together. True **or** False
8. Do you find yourself in an emotional outburst with muscle contractions or paralysis that you can link to an event that happened in your past? Yes **or** No
9. Are there particular events that are linked to or trigger trauma that you find humiliating and lonely? Yes **or** No
10. Do you remember bits and pieces of events that led to trauma from you without remembering it in a synchronized manner? Yes **or** No
11. Write out the bits and pieces of the event that caused you trauma as it comes to you. (it doesn't matter how long it takes for you to write it down)

____

____

____

____

____

____

12. How can you become better? Do you think talking with a therapist or a trusted friend or group can help? What can you do?

____

____

____

____

____

____

CHAPTER TWELVE: THE UNBEARABLE HEAVINESS OF REMEMBERING

A few points we learned in this chapter

Total memory loss is most common in childhood sexual abuse.

As long as memory is inaccessible, the mind is unable to change it.

The mind determines what you remember about trauma, it makes meaning of what it knows, and the meaning we make of our lives changes how and what we remember.

Traumatic memories are different from the stories we tell about the past

Core strengthening creates a sense of personal safety and mastery that helps the individual live in the present and keep the memories in the past so the future can emerge.

Answer the following questions sincerely

1. Did you ever feel you were never abused or experienced a trauma, and you later remember that it happened? Yes **or** No
2. How did you feel when you remembered?

____

____

____

____

____

____

3. What do you do when you can't remember the events that led to a trauma?

____

____

____

____

____

____

4. Do flashbacks from an event that caused trauma overwhelm you? Yes **or** No
5. Have you ever experienced a trauma, and you have never been able to remember what happened? Yes **or** No
6. Culture shapes the expression of traumatic stress. True **or** False
7. Your mind can twist the events that caused trauma. True **or** False
8. Finding the words to describe what happened to you can be transformative, and it boosts your concentration and makes sure you don't feel the pain linked to the memory of the trauma. True **or** False
9. Do you feel you live dual lives since after a trauma? Yes **or** No
10. How do you think you can become better? By Pilates, dance class, or social support? Mention them

____

____

____

____

____

____

PART FIVE: PATHS TO RECOVERY

CHAPTER THIRTEEN: HEALING FROM TRAUMA: OWNING YOUR SELF

A few points we learned in this chapter

We can't undo the events that led to trauma; we can only deal with the imprints of trauma on the body, mind, and soul. Trauma robs you of the feeling that you're in charge of yourself. The challenge of recovery is the reestablishment of the ownership of your body and your mind- which is yourself. This is the way to be free from shame, being overwhelmed, rage, and similar emotions.

Understanding how you feel a certain way doesn't change how you feel, but it can prevent you from surrendering to intense reactions such as assaulting someone who reminds you of a trauma.

Recovery from trauma involves the restoration of executive functioning and the self-confidence and capacity for playfulness and creativity. This means we become aware of our inner experience and learn to befriend what is going on inside us.

Becoming aware of how your body organizes particular emotions or memories opens the possibility of releasing sensations and impulses you once blocked in order to survive.

Trauma therapists need to learn how-to techniques to stabilize and calm patients down, help to lay traumatic memories to rest, and reconnect the patients with the rest of the world.

Stress hormones are meant to give us the strength and endurance to respond to extraordinary conditions. Helplessness and immobilization keep people from utilizing their stress hormones to defend themselves.

Pendulation is gently moving in and out of accessing internal sensations and traumatic memories. This helps patients to gradually expand their window of tolerance.

When walking, don't bend or hang your head in shame. Walk with your shoulders upright and take note of your environment with the understanding that no one dares mess with you.

CBT helps patients deal with the tendency to avoid talking about trauma; it exposes patients to the stimulus without bad things happening, so they get less upset. This way, the bad memories will have become associated with corrective information of being safe.

Answer these questions sincerely and take the exercise

1. Cast your mind back to an event that caused you trauma that you have been able to talk about. Write it out.

____

____

____

____

____

____

2. When you were writing about it, was it just a story or a narrative or it came with emotional and physical sensations that you remember too vividly? Try to describe how you felt.

____

____

____

____

____

____

3. To regain control of yourself from trauma, you need to revisit the trauma. True **or** False
4. Post-traumatic reactions and sensations are located in the emotional brain. True **or** False
5. Do you feel alive when you're hugged, touched, patted, or rocked? Yes **or** No
6. Tick the ones that apply to you

These are the effect of trauma that I feel

- Tightness in my chest
- Breathing fast and shallow
- Gut-wrenching sensations
- Heart pounding
- Body trembling
- Speaking with an uptight and reedy voice
- Defensiveness
- Rage
- Headaches or migraine
- Muscle aches
- Emotional outbursts
- Anger
- I eat compulsively
- Others

7. The more stressed out we are, the more our rational brains remain dormant. True **or** False
8. How do you think you can become better? How can you get over the feelings and emotions that overwhelm you when the flashbacks come? By yoga, breathing exercising, tai chi, body movements such as dancing and drumming, martial arts (judo, jujitsu, taekwondo, aikido, and kendo) qigong, or chanting? Mention them

____

____

____

____

____

____

9. When experiencing physical sensations, pay attention to the thoughts that run through your mind. What particular thoughts produce different sensations? Are you thinking of a breakup or a rape or events from a war or any other distressing thought? Identify the particular thought.

____

____

____

____

____

____

10. The next time you feel your emotions taking over due to the feeling of trauma, try the following
    - Sit still
    - Take a deep breath and count 1 -10 in ascending and descending order. Do this a couple of times (which can be 5 times)
    - Label the emotions you feel. An example: 'my heart thumps when I feel nervous' or 'I feel a migraine when the flashbacks come.'
    - Notice how the sensation changes or lifts when you take a deep breath.
    - Take it easy and don't force anything.
11. Who is your friend? Who do you trust or share vital information with?

____

____

____

12. Do you keep relationships with family members, friends, loved ones, AA meetings, veterans' organizations, religious communities, or therapists? Yes **or** No
13. How do you feel when you're with them?

14. Do you feel comfortable with your therapist? Do you feel safe in the person's presence? Yes **or** No
15. Is your therapist judgmental, harsh, or stern? Yes **or** No

If yes, then the person may not be able to help you resolve your traumatic stress.

16. Does the presence or look of your therapist remind you of someone who hurt or abused you, or does the therapist make you feel suspicious? Yes **or** No

If yes, talk it through with your therapist; without this, there may be no real change.

17. Which of these would you like to try out to help you feel better when you're among a community?

- Taking part in a play
- Aiko
- Tango
- Rumba
- Kickboxing

18. If you're a therapist, what's the best way to reach out to your client for the first time? Would you attempt a handshake? How do you shake the client?

CHAPTER FOURTEEN: LANGUAGE: MIRACLE AND TYRANNY

A few points we learned in this chapter

While trauma keeps us dumbfounded, the path out of it is caved with words, carefully assembled, piece by piece, until the whole story can be revealed. Feeling listened to and understood changes our psychology. As long as you keep secrets and suppress information, you're at war with yourself.

There are two distinct forms of self-awareness: one that keeps track of the self across time and one that registers the self in the present moment.

Answer the following questions sincerely and try out the exercise

1. Can you remember any trauma you went through that you had to talk about? Yes **or** No
2. How did you feel after talking about it?

____

____

____

____

____

____

3. Tick the ones that apply to you

After going through trauma, these are the thoughts that run through my mind

- I feel dead inside
- I will never be able to feel normal emotions again
- I have permanently changed for the worse
- I feel like an object, not a person
- I have no future. I feel like I don't know myself anymore

- Something is always wrong with me

4. Full communication is the opposite of being traumatized. True **or** False
5. It is easier to talk generally about anything than to talk about my feelings to others. Yes **or** No
6. All humans have two selves: there's an autobiographic self, and there's every-moment self-awareness. True **or** False
7. Writing helps to connect the self-observing parts and narrative parts of the brain without worrying about the reception you'll get. True **or** False
8. Have you ever written a letter to yourself? Yes **or** No
9. If you did, were you able to connect with yourself better? Yes **or** No
10. Write a letter to yourself about anything that happened yesterday

____

____

____

____

____

____

11. Write a letter to yourself about the happiest thing you've ever experienced. After writing it, go over it to see if you can connect with the emotions you feel
12. Do you think writing about your experiences helps? If yes, why? If no, why not?

____

____

____

____

____

____

13. How do you think you can be better in the next six months? By drawing, dancing, writing, drumming, or a combination of all? Mention them

____
____
____
____
____
____

14. To overcome trauma, you need help to get back in touch with your body. True **or** False
15. Keep a journal with you at all times. Write about an image of the flashback that comes to your mind. Don't force it, just write as it comes to you

CHAPTER FIFTEEN: LETTING GO OF THE PAST: EMDR

A few points we learned in this chapter

EMDR: Eye Movement Desensitization and Reprocessing. It helps to make painful re-creations of the trauma a thing of the past. It allows the patient to stay fully focused on their internal experience with sometimes extraordinary results.

EMDR has the capacity to activate a series of unsought and seemingly unrelated sensations, emotions, images, and thoughts in conjunction with the original memory.

Increasing our time in REM sleep reduces depression; the less REM sleep we get, the more likely we are to become depressed. PTSD is associated with disturbed sleep, and self-medication with alcohol or drugs further disrupts REM sleep.

The sleeping brain can make sense out of information whose relevance is unclear while we are awake and integrate it into the larger memory system.

Dreams keep replaying, recombining, and reintegrating pieces of old memories for months and even years. They regularly update the subterranean realities that determine what our waking minds pay attention to.

Drugs can blunt the images and sensations of terror, but they remain embedded in the mind and body

Answer the following questions sincerely

1. EMDR helps the brain unknot memories from the past. True **or** False
2. EMDR helps people heal from trauma as they talk about it. True **or** False
3. EMDR makes sure people have an open and understanding hear. True **or** False

4. Have you ever gone for an EMDR session before? Yes **or** No
5. How many EMDR sessions have you attended

____

____

____

6. If yes, how did you feel after each session?

____

____

____

____

____

____

7. What can you do to step out of the trauma in the past and live in the present? Is it EMDR, Yoga, journaling, or CBT? Mention them

____

____

____

____

____

____

8. Have you ever woken up from a sound sleep, and the images of a trauma come back to you? Yes **or** No
9. How do you feel after you had a good sleep?

____

____

____

____

____

____

10. Do you get depressed or moody when you don't sleep well? Yes **or** No
11. Have you been able to put different images of an event or trauma together with the help of different dreams?
    Yes **or** No

CHAPTER SIXTEEN: LEARNING TO INHABIT YOUR BODY: YOGA

A few points we learned from this chapter

The autonomic nervous system regulates arousal in the body. While the sympathetic nervous system uses chemicals like adrenaline to fuel the body and brain to take action. And the parasympathetic nervous system uses acetylcholine to help regulate basic body functions such as digestion, healing wounds, and sleep and dream cycles.

Good heart rate variability is a measure of well-being. Poor heart rate variability, which is a lack of fluctuation in heart rate, negatively affects how we think, how we feel, and the body's response to stress.

Changing the way one breathes can solve problems of anger, depression, and anxiety. Yoga can positively influence high blood pressure, elevated stress hormone secretion, asthma, and low back pain.

Yoga programs consist of breath practices (*pranayama*), stretches or postures (*asanas*), and meditation. The focus is on helping participants notice which muscles are active at different times.

We do not truly know ourselves unless we can feel and interpret our physical sensations; we need to register and act on these sensations to navigate safely through life

Answer the following questions and take the exercises where necessary

1. The body's nervous system works optimally when we are comfortable within ourselves and with our bodies.
   True **or** False
2. Inhalation helps to stimulate the ANS and increases the heart rate while exhalation helps to stimulate the SNS and the pace of the heartbeat. True **or** False

3. Effective arousal modulation gives us control over our impulses and emotions. True **or** False
4. Do you feel disoriented or disturbed so much that it affects certain parts of your body such as your head, your back, your neck, your waist, or other parts of your body? Yes **or** No
5. Mention the parts in which you feel the disintegration or disorientation

____

____

____

____

____

____

6. Do you feel numb afterward? If yes, how do you make the numbing go away? Do you cut yourself, take drugs, binge on foods or sugar, get angry, have emotional outbursts, gamble, take substantial amounts of alcohol, or get involved in sex and prostitution? Mention what you do.

____

____

____

____

____

____

7. Do you take breathing exercises? Yes **or** No
8. Does breathing help you feel better within yourself? Do you feel like you own your body when you take breathing exercises? How do you feel when you take breathing exercises?

____

____

____

____

9. Have you ever tried out yoga? Yes **or** No
10. How did you feel afterward? Did you feel in charge of your body, or were you able to communicate and listen to your body? Can you explain how it felt?

11. Which of the yoga poses has been the most difficult for you to try out, and why?

12. Has it been difficult to relax and get to the point of bliss and safe surrender after you experienced a trauma? Yes **or** No
13. How do you think you can get better? Is it through yoga, breathing exercises, or dancing? Mention the ways you can better

When you wake up, sit still without moving. Take in deep breaths and lift your hands gently from the side as you take in deep breaths. Drop your hands gently as you let out the air. Try to do this for about twenty to thirty minutes after you wake up and right before you sleep. While you do it, focus on your breathing (you can focus on your out-breaths in the morning), feel your feet on the floor and be aware of the rise and fall of your chest.

CHAPTER SEVENTEEN: PUTTING THE PIECES TOGETHER: SELF-LEADERSHIP

A few points we learned in this chapter

Pushing away intense feelings can be highly adaptive in the short run. It may help you preserve your dignity and independence; it may help you maintain focus on critical tasks, but the problems always show up later.

Just as we need to revisit traumatic memories to integrate them, we need to revisit the parts of ourselves that developed the defensive habits that helped us survive.

How well we get along with ourselves depends largely on our internal leadership skills – how well we listen to our different parts, make sure they feel taken care of, and keep them from sabotaging one another. Parts come as absolute when, in fact, they represent only one element in a constellation of thoughts, emotions, and sensations.

Every primary school of psychology recognizes that people have subpersonalities and gives them different names.

The parts of the mind form a network or system in which change in any one part will affect all the others. We all have parts that are childlike and fun, but when we are abused, these are the parts that are hurt the most; they become frozen, carrying the pain terror, and betrayal of abuse. The burden makes them toxic – parts of ourselves that we need to deny at all costs. This burden makes them toxic – parts of ourselves that we deny at all costs. They are called exiles.

The Fire-fighters are emergency responders that act impulsively whenever an experience triggers an emotion. They will destroy the house to extinguish the fire.

It's the managers who tell you to grin and bear it. That's the part that says I'm fine.

Answer the following questions sincerely and take the exercise

1. Trauma injects parts of the mind with beliefs and emotions that hijack them out of their naturally viable state.
   True **or** False
2. In trauma, the self-system breaks down, and parts of the self become polarized and go to war with one another.
   True **or** False
3. Recognizing that each part is stuck with burdens makes it feel less threatening. True **or** False
4. Do you feel you have multiple personalities? Yes **or** No
5. Tick the following as it applies to you

- There are different parts of me
- There's a part of me that likes excitement and wants to live at the edge of the world
- There's a part of me that's sad and gloomy
- There's a part of me that's a fearful little child
- There's a part of me that snaps and is given to emotional outbursts
- There's a part of me that wants to be carefree and playful
- There's a part of me that's always angry
- There's a part of me that's vulnerable but doesn't want to be seen
- I'm sure there are other parts still within me

6. Can you identify when each of these parts comes out? What triggers it? What makes you get angry? Is it when you're trying to protect yourself from becoming vulnerable?

____

____

____

____

7. If a part of you that you don't like comes to the fore or wants to become noticeable, what do you do? Do you take drugs, work out at the gym, have sex, take alcohol? Mention them

____
____
____
____
____
____

8. Do you have outbursts, or do you react spontaneously when something unexpected happens to you? Yes **or** No
9. Do you get surprised at your reaction? Are you shocked where that part of you came from? Yes **or** No
10. Do you practice mindfulness? Yes **or** No
11. If yes, how do you feel after each session?

____
____
____
____
____
____

12. Practicing mindfulness

The first thing you need is a place. It must be comfortable and convenient; most of all, it should be quiet so you can easily quiet down and calm down easily. Sit down comfortably.

If you're a beginner, you may not be able to quieten your mind for too long. Begin with a short time, which can be 5 to 10 minutes.

Pay attention to your body and notice the pattern of your breath and watch your body rise and fall in line with your breath.

It's normal for your mind to wander within a few seconds; bring it back to the present whenever it does. Don't be discouraged; rather, keep at it. As your attention span gets better, increase the time frame for meditation.

CHAPTER EIGHTEEN: FILLING IN THE HOLES: CREATING STRUCTURES

A few points we learned in this chapter

Psychomotor therapy doesn't explain or interpret the past. Instead, it allows you to feel what you felt back then, to visualize what you saw, and to say what you could not say when it happened.

Feeling safe means you can say things to people who have hurt you at one point in time. For example, you can say things to your father or rather the placeholder who represents him that you wish you could have said as a five-year-old. You can experiment with distance and proximity and explore what happens as you move placeholders around.

As you take charge of representing the reality of your experience, the witness keeps you company, reflecting the changes in your posture, facial expression, and tone of voice.

Nobody grows up under ideal circumstances – as if we even know what ideal circumstances are. But we know that in order to become self-confident and capable adults, it helps enormously to have grown up with steady and predictable parents: parents who delight in you, in your discoveries and explorations, parents who helped you organize your comings and goings, and who served as role models for self-care and getting along with other people.

If your map of the world is based on trauma, abuse, and neglect, people are likely to seek shortcuts to oblivion.

In order to change, people need to become viscerally familiar with realities that directly contradict the static feelings of the frozen or panicked self or trauma, replacing them with sensations rooted in safety, mastery, delight, and connection.

Answer the following questions sincerely and practice the exercises where necessary

1. Trauma makes people to interpret the present from the past. True **or** False
2. Recreating structures in a structure helps you see the structure of your inner world, and you can restructure your past and the map in your brain. True **or** False
3. The healing tableaus of structures offer an experience that many participants have never believed was possible for them to get into a world where they feel safe and protected. True **or** False
4. Were trauma, abuse, and neglect a part of your life when growing up? Yes **or** No
5. Did you always expect rejection and ridicule? Yes **or** No
6. Did you feel that you are incapable of loving or being loved? Yes **or** No
7. Do you feel that you're intrinsically a bad person and don't deserve any respect? Yes **or** No
8. If yes, can you link certain events that happened that made you conclude on that?

____

____

____

____

____

____

9. Imagine a little child that was your age when you went through trauma was there with you. He or she is going through the same experiences that made you conclude that you're a bad person, you're unloved, and you deserve no respect. What would you tell this child? Will you tell him it's normal to go through these experiences, or she deserved what she got? Would you give her a hug or tell him he deserved better? What would you say?

____

____

10. Try out this exercise

- Write out the names of everyone who was linked to a trauma you developed when you were a child.
- Pick up vases or jars with lids and write each person's name on each jar
- Write a letter to each one of them telling them how you truly feel. Put each person's letter in the jar.
- After a few days or when you feel better, pick up each letter and read it out loud to the vase. Replace each letter in each vase and dispose the vase.

CHAPTER NINETEEN: REWIRING THE BRAIN: NEUROFEEDBACK

A few points we learned in this chapter

Neurofeedback is similar to watching someone's face during a conversation. If you see smiles or slight nods, you're rewarded, and you go on telling your story, but when your conversation partner is bored, you'll start to wrap up or change the topic.

Patients need help to change the habitual brain patterns created by trauma and its aftermath. When the fear patterns relax, the brain becomes less susceptible to automatic stress reactions and can focus better on ordinary events.

Neurofeedback changes brain connectivity patterns; the mind follows by creating new patterns of engagement

Alpha-theta training is a wonderful neurofeedback procedure because it can be used to induce the sorts of hypnagogic states which is the essence of hypnotic trance

Answer the following questions sincerely

1. Neurofeedback can be used to intervene in the circuitry that promotes and sustains states of fear and traits of fearfulness, shame, and rage. True **or** False
2. Stress is triggered by events. True **or** False
3. Neurofeedback stabilizes the brain and increases resiliency, allowing us to develop more choices in how to respond.
   True **or** False

4. Have you ever felt better when you decided to go off meds that were made to make you feel better? Yes **or** No
5. Did you get tired of meds and search for an alternative? Yes **or** No
6. Have you ever tried neurofeedback to treat trauma? Yes **or** No
7. Do you think neurofeedback can fill in the gaps and connect events that lead to trauma to pleasure activities or activities in the present? Yes **or** No
8. Tick the following as it applies to you

- Neurofeedback leads to a deep sense of comfort
- Neurofeedback brings balance to the moods and emotions
- It allows individuals to express themselves in clear language
- It brings self-awareness
- With neurofeedback, I sleep better
- Neurofeedback makes me feel calm
- It sharpens my focus
- Neurofeedback boosts creativity
- It helps to reverse learning disabilities
- It gives me a new perspective on my life
- It feels absolutely weird, and I dread it
- It relieves tension and anxiety
- It reduced my blood pressure
- It helped me reflect on good and love
- I can be sexually intimate since I began neurofeedback

9. What other benefits can you associate with neurofeedback?

____

____

____

____

____

10. Alpha waves brain links the word within an individual with the world surrounding the individual. Yes **or** No
11. Since you began neurofeedback, have you experienced more or fewer arousal patterns? Yes **or** No
12. When you are trying to douse tension or stop the tension that comes with trauma, what would you do? Take alcohol, have sex, take drugs, EMDR, neurofeedback? What would you do?

____

____

____

____

____

13. How can you become better within the next one year? Would you attempt neurofeedback, dance, yoga, EMDR? What options will you be willing to attempt? Mention them?

____

____

____

____

CHAPTER TWENTY: FINDING YOUR VOICE: COMMUNAL RHYTHMS AND THEATER

A few points we learned in this chapter

Unlike therapy and therapists, theater allows individuals to be someone other than someone with a disability or problem but as someone who has something to contribute and opens the door to creativity.

Our sense of urgency, how much we feel in control, is defined by our relationship with our bodies, and it's rhythms. Acting is an experience of using your body to take place in life.

Music binds together people who might individually be terrified but who collectively become powerful advocates for themselves and others.

Traumatized people are terrified to think deeply because they are afraid to experience their emotions. Since these emotions lead to loss of control. In contrast, the theater is about embodying emotions, giving voice to them, becoming rhythmically engaged, taking on, and embodying different roles.

In theater, props and costumes help the participants take risks in new roles as they can lighten up from the playful atmosphere and support from their fellow actors.

In the theater program, the first rehearsal establishes basic agreements: responsibility, accountability, and respect. In the second phase, they learn to share life's stories.

Answer the following questions sincerely

1. Theater gives the opposite of dissociation as you are in tune with your body and love your body. True **or** False
2. Theater functions are the opposite of the trauma effect. True **or** False
3. Collective movement and music create a larger context for our lives. True **or** False
4. Theater programs teach cause and effect. True **or** False
5. Music, language, dancing, marching, and singing can't give trauma victims courage, hope, or the ability to dream. Yes **or** No
6. Tick the below as it applies to you

- Theater helps me connect with other people
- Theater helps me understand the story of people around me
- Since I began theater, it has been easier to resolve conflicts
- Theater helps me express my emotions better
- Theater helps me hide myself better
- I love theater because I find myself in another world free from trauma
- Theater makes me feel strong within
- Theater helps me question my paradigm and find new paradigms
- It helps me deal with trauma triggers
- It helps me manage trauma re-enactments

7. Have you ever participated in theater before? Yes **or** No

8. Was it easy to make eye contact with people?

   Yes **or** No

9. What was the most challenging role you ever had to play?

____

____

____

____

____

____

10. Why was it difficult?

____

____

____

____

____

____

11. How different was that role from what you go through daily?

____

____

____

____

____

____

12. In theater, I have learned to question everything around me, especially my view of the world. It teaches me to look out for other people's opinions in life. Yes **or** No
13. Would you rather take alcohol, take drugs or substances, engage in compulsive sex, or participate in theater programs? Why?

____

____

____

____

____

____

14. Have you been able to make a friend or say hi to an acquaintance every time you go for your theater programs? Yes **or** No
15. If yes, how did it happen?

____

____

____

____

____

____

Made in the USA
Coppell, TX
25 October 2022

85225913R00037